bacchae

a collection of essays edited by
david stuttard and tamsin shasha

aod publications • brighton

published by
aod publications

© **aod** 2006

actors of dionysus,
14 cuthbert road, brighton, uk bn2 0en

t: +0044 1273 692 604
f: +0044 1273 692 604
e: info@actorsofdionysus.com
www.actorsofdionysus.com

cover photograph: **aod** after Bacchae at Ephesus
photograph by Dave Ashton

aod publications

essays on bacchae

Essays on Bacchae is published in association with **aod** (Actors of Dionysus), the UK's leading theatre company dedicated to classical Greek drama.

Founded in 1993 by David Stuttard and Tamsin Shasha, **aod** eschews a traditional "archaeological" approach, seeking to bring the plays vividly alive for a modern generation and working with practitioners such as Marcello Magni from Theatre de Complicité and Thea Barnes from Phoenix Dance.

aod tours regularly throughout the British Isles and has performed in Greece, Turkey and Croatia.

In addition to productions and publications, **aod** runs a strong educational programme, including workshops and summer schools. Talks are given before certain performances by leading scholars, many of whom have contributed to this collection of essays.

aod has broadcast on BBC Radio 3, and its audiobook of Medea was released worldwide by Penguin in 1997. The Independent described Tamsin Shasha's performance in the central role as "chillingly convincing", while The Financial Times said that the performances "make it clear why the Greeks were so excited about this play more than a millennium ago".

aod's stage performances have been described by The Guardian as "direct and accessible", by The Irish Times as "perfectly pitched" and by The Yorkshire Evening Press as "seriously sexy", while The Times wrote that "they perform these ancient stories with such conviction that they bring tears to the eyes and make the hair at the nape of the neck bristle. Let nothing stop you from seeing them!"

Tamsin Shasha trained at Oxford School of Drama.and L'Ecole Philippe Gaulier. Co-founded **aod** in 1993 and for them has worked extensively as performer, director, producer, workshop teacher and movement coach, collaborating with Thea Barnes (formerly Artistic Director Phoenix Dance) on *Medea* 2002 and Marcello Magni (founder member Complicite) on *Oedipus* 2003. For Penguin Audiobooks, in collaboration with **aod** she performed the part of Medea for the worldwide launch of their new Drama series. She directed the National tour of *Trojan Women* in 2005 and will soon direct their National revival of *Oedipus*. A skilled aerialist, she has recently collaborated with Brighton's Circus Project and BandBazi on *The Persian Cinderella* and *Breakfast at Audrey's* respectively. She is currently writing her first solo performance piece, *Bacchic* inspired by *The Bacchae* and working with rope.

David Stuttard studied Classics at St. Andrews University and subsequently taught in Edinburgh, St. Andrews and York. In 1993, he co-founded **aod**, for which he directed his own translations and adaptations of Greek tragedies. In addition to stage shows, he produced the Penguin Audiobook of *Medea* and a video, *The Face of Tragedy*, while his play *Blow Your Mind, Aristophanes!* premiered at London''s Mermaid Theatre in association with the British Film Institute and Channel 4. His work has been heard on BBC Radio 3, and his translation of Aeschylus' Agamemnon is an Open University set text. David has produced plays for performance in ancient theatres in Turkey and Albania, including Troy, Ephesus, Aspendus and Butrint. In 2005, with his new Company Dionysus he recorded a cd performance of *Trojan Women*. The author of *An Introduction to Trojan Women*, he is currently writing a dramatic reconstruction of *Alexandros* and *Palamedes*, two lost plays by Euripides. You can contact him via his website, www.davidstuttard.com

Foreword

Bacchae is a haunting play, a play which gets under your skin. For **aod**, it has a particular resonance - and not only because its central character is Dionysus. Our production in 2000 was singularly successful, and it was this play that we first performed at Ephesus.

Part of what makes the play so special is the way in which Euripides manipulates the audience, so that for the first half (if not more) we are completely seduced by Dionysus, relishing his humiliation of the puritanical Pentheus, and completely at one with his desire for revenge. But it becomes brutally clear that, like Pentheus, we have been duped by Dionysus, carried along on a tide of blind infatuation, complicit in what we eventually realise is an unspeakable orgy of violence and death.

But despite its unarguably grisly story-line, *Bacchae*, like Dionysus himself, is unforgettably exuberant, playful and primitive.

If the play contains paradoxes and problems, so do the circumstances of its composition and our reception of the text.

It is an apparently profoundly religious work by a writer known in his own age as an arch-agnostic, composing in seemingly self-imposed exile from his native Athens. But for what audience was he writing - Athens, in the doomed twilight of its experiment with democracy, or his new home, fiercely monarchic Macedonia, where, two generations later, a new self-styled Dionysus would be born to conquer the world? Or was his audience more universal? What does that say about his vision?

And what *can* we say about his vision, when a crucial passage at the end of the play has been lost? In our own production of the play, we exploited the fact that Euripides' ending was lost to create our own, which showed Dionysus as a figure as ambiguous in victory as he had been in his struggle, suspended between heaven and earth, neither truly god nor truly man - the charismatic performer exposed as a lonely, angst-ridden outsider.

For a performer, you can make of what is lost what you will. For a scholar and an academic, however, it is yet one more problem to be solved.

Tamsin and I are most grateful to all those scholars who have contributed to this collection for their commitment and enthusiasm, to Mavis MacDougall, who has read and commented wisely on the essays, to Alison Fewings in the **aod** office, to John and Stan at Hamilton Printing, Hull for their patience, help and advice - and to EJ Birtwell and Mark Katz for their support, understanding and good-humour.

David Stuttard
Brighton, August 2003

Contents

The contributors

Sir Kenneth Dover is Chancellor of the University of St. Andrews

Carmel McCallum Barry lectures in the Department of Ancient Classics at University College, Cork

David Raeburn, formerly lectured at New College, Oxford, and regularly directs Greek tragedies at Cambridge and Bradfield

Alan Sommerstein is Professor of Greek at the University of Nottingham

Richard Seaford is Professor of Greek at the University of Exeter

Pat Easterling is Professor of Greek at Newnham College, Cambridge

Alex Garvie is emeritus Professor of Greek at the University of Glasgow

bacchae

the bacchus leaps high
and smoke billows
like frankincense
trailed from his pine torch

he dances
he dances

there's none won't dance with him now
wild with his bacchic cries
head
thrown back
hair
blowing free in the breeze

his dancers scream loud
and he answers in thunder
go bacchae
now bacchae

embrace dionysus
and dance in the wind
like the gold dust of tmolus
drumming the rhythm
ecstatic
exalting god
gasping
in ecstasy
gasping
the lotus flute throbbing
in ecstasy
joining its voice
to the voice of the dancers

go to the mountains
the mountains

and
like a colt
straining its limbs
its swift hooves
in the meadows
galloping close
to its mother
exultant

like a colt
all exultant
the dancer leaps high

A Versatile God

Sir Kenneth Dover

In the closing years of the Fifth Century BCE the Theatre of Dionysus at Athens witnessed productions of two plays – one tragedy and one comedy – in which the god in whose honour they were performed had the leading role. The comedy was Aristophanes' *Frogs*, datable with certainty to the beginning of 405; the tragedy was Euripides' *Bacchae*, one of three plays which their author's death in 407/6 left for his son to produce. It is quite possible that *Bacchae* and *Frogs* were performed on the same occasion, but it would be hard to find in any pair of plays two so fundamentally divergent treatments of the same character.

Euripides' Dionysus is as formidable as only the son of a god by a mortal woman can be. Such "half-breeds" were normally what the Greeks called "heroes" and "heroines", worshipped with offerings where they were deemed to have been buried. But Dionysus, like Herakles, was one of the exceptions, admitted to the society of Olympus as a god with a god's powers. One of these powers is that of infusing into mortals of both sexes and all ages a tireless energy and a prodigious physical strength (the ability to tear a large, struggling mammal limb from limb with one's bare hands requires divine help). Stone walls and locks and bolts cannot constrain the god; nor can human will and sense, for he can impose on us whatever delusions he wishes. And for the sustenance of his worshippers he can make rocks and earth spout water, wine, milk and honey. Moreover, he has in full measure some of the most disagreeable features of divine personality: he is insatiable for honour, proud, vindictive, recklessly unjust in punishment. In the last

1

scene of the play Kadmos dares to reproach him, saying that gods should be better than mortals in temper. But Dionysus is unmoved by that, saying only that Zeus sanctioned what he has done.

But look now at the Dionysus of *Frogs*. A god, for sure, and a son of Zeus, but seemingly with his divine powers in abeyance. He is most like a character in a sitcom, a person to whom things happen rather than one who decides what shall happen to others. Xanthias, the slave who accompanies him on his journey to the underworld in order to carry his luggage, as a human slave would attend a human master on a journey, say, from Marathon to Eleusis, can fairly be called a faithful servant, but (like many a faithful servant) knows how to look after Number One. He describes his master as an easy-going guy whose interests and talents are limited to "drinking and fucking". Certainly when the toughness and endurance of master and slave are put to the test, it is the slave who appears to advantage. Faced with the threats of the angry, bellowing doorkeeper of the underworld, Dionysus loses control of his bowels and has to be cleaned up. Throughout the contest between the ghost of Aeschylus and the ghost of Euripides, a contest which he is required (having unrivalled experience as a spectator of dramatic performances) to decide, he is, as Rosemary Harriott put it , "sometimes acting the fool and always foolish".

There are no doubt cultures in which two such radically irreconcilable representations of one and the same god can coexist. In the time of the Reformation and its very long-lived aftermath, gross and venomous pictures, verses and pamphlets were freely used in conflicts over doctrine, liturgy and authority, and we might for a moment contemplate the possibility that we have before us a vehement religious disagreement between Euripides and Aristophanes. Did Euripides hope to (so to speak) save the souls of his audience, while Aristophanes, a happy sceptic, wished only to raise a laugh from kindred spirits, both poets expressing their individual attitudes to religious faith? Or could it be that Euripides, adopting a standpoint which we know was given an emphatic expression by the poet Xenophanes a century earlier, struck a blow against conventional religion by forcing us to confront the violence and cruelty of accepted myths and letting us settle in our consciences the disturbing question, "Can *gods* really have behaved in this monstrous way?"

One thing of which we can be sure is that the festivals of Dionysus, to which the performance of tragedies and comedies alike belonged, were not the sort of occasion which resembled a seminar for earnest, patient and tolerant theologians seeking truth. Athenian attitudes to the search for truth are better glimpsed from the minor characters in Socratic dialogues than from Socrates himself. When historians of our own day encounter a problem in the interpretation of Greek religion, the first indispensable step is to shake free of modern concepts of "belief", "believe in ...", and "faith". A step of almost equal importance is to remember that in the post-Hellenic era, a large part of the human race has regarded certain narratives about the past as divinely inspired and therefore as necessarily true. Religious institutions have incorporated those narratives in sacred texts and have disseminated them widely. The Greek world, however, was fragmented to a degree quite extraordinary by comparison with our own, and each of the political units which collectively constituted it had traditions, rituals and usages not shared with other units. Since that fragmentation goes back to the preliterate stage of Greek culture, we should expect to find competing, irreconcilable versions of the same narrative, often reflecting no less irreconcilable concepts; and that is just what we do find. Within a given city-state the population is not united by theological doctrine or ecclesiastical authority, but by ceremonial usage, sacrifice and ritual; those are the practices through which the community maintains the goodwill of the gods by honouring them and looks for prosperity as the reward for honour.

To take an agnostic view of inherited narrative, i.e. of "myth", did not require intellectual effort, because the ordinary citizen attending public festivals, seeing plays and hearing choral or solo recitations of narrative poetry about deities and heroic ancestors, cannot have failed to notice that, although contradictory versions of the same myth could (logically) both be false, they could not (in common sense) both be true. One way of dealing with myths which gave trouble was simply to ignore them, or, when confronted with choice, to choose those versions of a myth which appealed most strongly to the aesthetic, moral, patriotic or familial preferences and loyalties of the chooser. But a hint at other grounds of choice appears in a striking passage of Herodotus concerning the conflicting versions of the story of Helen which were current from the mid-sixth century BCE onwards. One version was Homer's; in the other, Helen never arrived in Troy, but was detained in Egypt for the whole duration of the Trojan War. Herodotus declares his own adherence to the latter version, but adds that Homer rejected it because it was not as *euprepes* ("attractive", analysable as "looking good", "looking right") for epic poetry as the Homeric version.

The relative suitability of different myths (and different treatments of myth) to different art-forms is a consideration which we need to take into account in trying to reconcile the two Dionysi. The different versions of the Helen myth were *both* used by Euripides, one in *Trojan Women*, a wholly sombre play, in 415, and the other in *Helen*, a "happy ending" play, in 412. Since the cults and festivals of the Greek states evolved in their own way well before Greek became a written language, myth was not documented; hence Thucydides, in referring to the earliest inhabitants of Sicily (including the Cyclopses), declines to cite evidence and leaves it to us to see "what the poets have said" and use our "individual judgement". Hesiod represents the Muses as declaring, "We know how to tell much fiction that resembles truth, and we know – *when we wish* – to tell the truth."

How did the listener know when the Muses – and from their inspiration, the poets – wished to tell the truth? The poets in fact made good use of their licence to invent. It is Herodotus, again, who gives our theological assumptions a jolt by telling us that Aeschylus was the first poet ever to treat Artemis (and, I presume, her twin brother Apollo) as offspring not of Leto but of Demeter. So far as our evidence goes, no one adopted Aeschylus' idiosyncratic "view" of a "fact" enshrined in cult, poetry and the visual arts. And again – so far as our evidence goes – Aeschylus did not get into trouble; and Herodotus does not blame him as a "heretic", a "blasphemer", or as "impious".

Most deities can be beneficent, and all of them can be angry and punitive. The angry Dionysus is a personage who can play a frighteningly effective role in tragedy, and it is not surprising that *Bacchae* and

Pentheus are known to us as titles of plays by Aeschylus (possibly both titles denote the same play), and we hear too of a *Bacchae* by Sophocles' son Iophon, which may well be significantly earlier than Euripides' *Bacchae*, given that Iophon was active as a dramatist at least by 435. A comparable myth, that of the king Lycurgus who resisted the cult of Dionysus and was punished by an insanity which led him to kill his own family, was the material of a tetralogy by Aeschylus and of another by Polyphrasmon. It is a fair inference from the use made in Aristophanes, *Women at the Thesmophoria*, of a quotation from one or the other of those tetralogies that Lycurgus was portrayed as mocking the deceptively effeminate appearance of Dionysus as Pentheus does in *Bacchae*.

And just as the tragic Dionysus of Euripides had a literary ancestry, so did the comic Dionysus of Aristophanes. At least six relevant plays (by four different poets) preceded *Frogs*, and in at least two of them the god was presented as a laughable bungler, ambitious beyond the limits of his abilities and timid in the face of serious opponents. It seems that the god in whose honour the dramatic festivals were held was himself eligible for casting when either an Avenging Angel or a Pulcinello was required.

The Dionysus who appears so often in sixth-century and fifth-century vase-painting is in certain respects (not in all) a bridge between those two different aspects of the god. Most often he appears accompanied by satyrs (of whom we hear nothing in *Bacchae*) and by women dancing wildly and wielding the thyrsus, of which we hear so much in the play. Satyrs in vase-paintings in general were gross creatures, sexually insatiable and often drunk; the dancing women are *mainades*, "mad women", inspired and sustained by the power of the god. But the efforts of the satyrs (resisted by the *mainades*, who use their thyrsi in self-defence) fail to turn the dance into a sexual free-for-all; the vase-painting gives no support to the suspicious imagination of Pentheus. We have however reason, founded on non-literary evidence, to think that a giant model phallus figured in the procession at the City Dionysia (as it does in our own day in a comparable procession at Nagoya in Japan).

In certain parts of the Greek world there were "mysteries" of Dionysus, into which people could be "initiated" and acquire thereby the right to a much more agreeable life after death. The best evidence for these mysteries and their implication for the afterlife comes from Greek settlements in Italy. The behaviour of the bewitched and frenzied women of Thebes in *Bacchae* is commonly referred to as *telete*, and that is a word used especially of initiation procedures, but it is not exclusively so used; it can refer to religious rites of a less secret kind, and dancing in the hills does not appear in any other Athenian context as a requirement for initiation into a mystery. Athenian husbands did not have to worry that they would come home from the farm to find no one in the kitchen, but they would pretty certainly have been aware of the existence of Dionysiac mysteries, and Euripides' own awareness of it is an adequate explanation of his choice of words. Nevertheless, the god who plays so many divine roles had a foothold also in the Eleusinian Mysteries in so far as Iacchus, invoked in the procession to Eleusis, was also addressed as "Son of Semele" in a ritual cry at the festival of the Lenaia and is on occasion identified with Dionysus by poets (including Euripides at one point in *Bacchae*).

Vox populi, vox dei

Carmel McCallum Barry

Bacchae is for many people the most tragic of Greek tragedies, the most bleak and pessimistic in its unfolding. In its atmosphere of disintegration and monstrous images it has obvious affinities with Apocalypse literature of the Near East, in which portentous events raise the people of god into recognition amidst the downfall of rationality and social structures. **Bacchae** is especially unsettling and even frightening because the confrontation between divine and human is so immediate and face to face. But if we set this aspect aside it is clear that the pattern of plot and myth is not unusual in Greek tragedy. If we think only of plays connected with Thebes it is obvious that like Pentheus, men such as Oedipus, Creon and Eteocles are also rulers whose resistance to new or different perceptions of the world around them brings about their own downfall and that of their family. In such a scenario the pattern shows that the destruction of the ruling family is necessary for the continued survival of the city, therefore in *Bacchae* we need not think that the tragic end of Pentheus and his family means the end of civilisation too. There is no indication that the city of Thebes will be destroyed and we can presume that the people deserve to survive, to start again, without a self regarding royal family.

One of the unusual things about the play is the immediate presence of Dionysus. Often in Greek tragedy the god manipulates human destiny from the wings; separate in space and time he/she teases man with oracles and promises which cannot be understood fully until the tragic action is almost complete. But here Dionysus, most gentle and most terrible of gods, in person, now, makes his demand

'Worship me'. Men have no time to think about it, refusal or hesitation in acknowledging the divinity and his cult are instantly and terribly punished. It is this aspect of swift catastrophe which intensifies the tragic feel of the play.

The direct confrontation between man and god leads to another unusual feature, an added emphasis on other men in the play besides the heroic tragic protagonist. In the ideological struggle between Dionysus and Pentheus we do not find a chorus of men or women of Thebes agreeing in a soothing way with this speaker or that, but we see individual men of the city given a platform to express their thoughts on this contest between the two Theban cousins, the king and the god. They give us the people's view, a 'democratic' view, which they offer to Pentheus by way of advice; the fact that they survive and he does not demonstrates that their attitude is the right one. An examination of the roles of characters such as Teiresias, the palace servant and the herdsman will show that they are right because they recognise the workings of the divine will and accommodate themselves to it. Pentheus dies because he fails to recognise the importance of the city and the views of its citizens, and in the context of *Bacchae*'s composition and performance this would not have seemed unreasonable. At the time of the play's performance the city of Athens was itself close to dissolution, exhausted after many years of war and internal struggles, but it was still operating a democratic constitution. Citizens of the democracy enjoyed freedom of speech and action in personal affairs as well as financial and social support from the city. In return they were expected to serve the democracy, taking their turn as administrators, as soldiers, but all the time putting the interests of the city above personal interest. If we consider Pentheus' behaviour in these terms he is not a good ruler or a good citizen. An Athenian audience would expect that all men should be heard and that the majority opinion should prevail, therefore they would take an interest in the attitudes and reactions of the citizens of Thebes to the new religion. In the first part of the play, before Pentheus' mind is totally taken over by the god, these men (two of them at length) present their view of the situation to Pentheus, advising him on the best course of action. Their presentations are part of a democratic process; we can compare them to orators advising the Assembly. In this instance the voice of god and the voice of the people are in agreement, and so it is possible for the life of the city to continue. The people as a whole are not punished because, unlike the royal family, they recognise the need to worship Dionysus, and accept him without resistance. The main exponents of other views are Teiresias, the blind prophet whose job it is to interpret the will of god to men, and a messenger, a herdsman. Cadmus and a palace guard also speak briefly in support of the new religion. Their reactions to the god's demand for worship and to the rituals draw attention to Pentheus' behaviour and his wilful refusal to consider the situation in a rational way.

The insults to Dionysus have originated in the royal family, since Pentheus' mother, Agave, and his aunts proudly refused to accept that their sister Semele was loved by a god and gave birth to a god. They insisted that she conceived a child by a mortal man and that their father Cadmus concealed the shame by claiming Zeus was the father of her child; they also claim that Semele was killed by Zeus' thunderbolt because she lied about her love affair with him. Dionysus takes his revenge for this insult by liberating the women of Thebes, driving them (together with his aunts) out of the city to roam wild as Bacchants, on Mount Cithaeron close by. The contemporary audience would be alert to the significance of this extraordinary situation since in Athenian society of the time women were not counted as citizens, had few public functions and were expected to spend most of their time within the house. The god has attacked the stability of the city by subverting its basic unit, the *oikos*, or household, which includes family members and property as well as the household space. If the women make off for an alternative lifestyle in the hills there is no one to oversee the general organisation of the *oikos*, to do the washing and weaving, not to mention provide for its continuance by bearing legitimate children. Greek tragedy and myth supply many examples of the ever present anxiety that women who wander away from their homes may end up with illegitimate children that they have to abandon, palm off on their husbands or ascribe to some god.

So the fact that the women of Thebes have left the city and are roaming wild on the mountain is a catastrophe for the state, it indicates that the whole civic order is in danger of dissolution. "This city must learn well, even if unwilling, what it is to be without a share in my bacchic rituals," says Dionysus, (39) and he warns that if there is an attempt to bring back the Bacchant women from the mountain by force of arms, then he himself will join the battle. It is tragically inevitable that Pentheus, after his entrance, immediately decides on the very actions that the god has warned against. His reaction is a violent one; some of the women have already been captured and imprisoned and he intends to hunt down the rest and chain them up. He is horrified that they have left their homes to celebrate the bacchic rituals on the mountain, rituals which he assumes consist of drunken sexual orgies. Pentheus clearly recognises that the women's abandonment of their homes is a crisis for the city and for his claim to rule, since basic conventions of city life in family and religious organisation no longer operate. As he struggles to maintain civic order in the face of a disruptive religious cult, the battle between king and god in a sense is a familiar one, the clash between the authority of the state and the religious freedom of its subjects.

But Pentheus' downfall is not just a result of the god's wish to revenge an insult, it is also a result of his own failure to perceive what is necessary for the good of the city as a whole. We must not lose sight of the personal dimension of this contest either, because, as often in Greek tragedy, the deadly conflict is between members of the same family.

In contrast to Pentheus with his rash and unconsidered reactions, the other men of Thebes observe and reflect on what they have seen; their exchanges with him show their own sensible attitude and provide a commentary and judgement on the king's character. Their view is that the wisest, not just the most expedient course for the well being of the community is to subscribe to the new cult and that Pentheus is not a good thing for the city of Thebes, as a ruler or as a citizen. So his downfall although horrific, is inevitable, since his removal is necessary for the common good.

First to speak their opinions are the senior citizens; Teiresias and Cadmus, the former king, appear after the chorus of Dionysus' followers has finished its song about the joyful Bacchic rituals with a rousing exhortation to dance to the wild music like a foal leaping around its mother. The sight of the old men immediately afterwards, tottering on wearing all the trappings of the Bacchic cult and prepared despite their age to take part in the ecstatic dancing that the cult demands, must surely have raised a laugh. They intend to join the rituals on the mountain, but so far are the only men in the city who have decided to worship Dionysus in this way, "We alone have sense" says Teiresias declaring the significance of their action as clearly as the god himself would. The undignified, even ludicrous, aspect of old men dressing as Bacchants and dancing wildly is unimportant and irrelevant, as the god requires the same worship from all, young and old alike. When

Pentheus arrives, ranting violently against the Bacchants and their priest, the appearance of the older men makes him even more angry. He finds the sight of his grandfather in bacchic gear shameful and he reprimands him as an old man without a mind or without sense, a contradiction of Teiresias' assessment of what they are doing. Towards the prophet, Pentheus is more peremptory, accusing him of promoting the new religion in order to profit from increases in sacrificial revenues. Teiresias' well ordered reply is striking for its rationality, in total contrast to Pentheus' spluttering fury. The debate between the three men hinges on this very point of reason and good sense; is it Pentheus who possesses sense and the right (attitude of) mind, or the old men? As for Pentheus himself, Teiresias says he can speak well, but has no sense in his words, is a bad member of the *polis* and has no mind or power of analysis, *nous* (266-71).

His lack of sense and his failure as a citizen mean that Pentheus is doomed, as he is politically dangerous. Teiresias tries to persuade the king with some reasoned arguments to accept the god since he confers benefits on mankind; just as Demeter bestows corn, the dry part of man's necessary food, so Dionysus supplies the moist necessities, and wine in particular. He goes on to explain the nature of the divine birth and Dionysus' role for mankind in similar intellectual and fashionable terms. Human behaviour and the god's demands can be rationalised too; he argues that the god does not make women unchaste, they are by nature either chaste or not, and also, that since it is natural for Pentheus to desire worship as a king it is reasonable for Dionysus as a god to require it too.

Rational argument is not very successful with Pentheus, so Teiresias also produces more serious warnings of the dangers involved in opposition to the new religion. The warnings emphasise the power of the bacchic madness which forms part of the cult, and also that Dionysus is powerful in arms and battle, and will prevail, even in the cult places of established religion like Delphi. This is the kind of warning that any ruler should listen to when it comes from a prophet who claims to speak for god to the people. But Pentheus, like Oedipus, another hot headed ruler, both sees and does not see, whereas the blind Teiresias can see the truth more clearly than other men.

The other old man, Cadmus, approves of and adds to the prophet's words, but from a different perspective, for while Teiresias speaks for honouring the god, Cadmus is concerned for the honour of the royal house of Thebes. He too tells Pentheus that he has no sense, but his advice to him is not the wholehearted acceptance of the god that Teiresias advocates. Cadmus advises his grandson to do what is politic and expedient; even if he doesn't believe that Dionysus is a god, he should pretend that he is, so that their family will gain honour. He warns him to remember the fate of his cousin Actaeon, who offended the goddess Artemis and was torn to pieces by his own hunting dogs. This is obviously prophetic but also has a family relevance. Even though Cadmus takes part in the rituals of the new religion, his prime concern remains the honour of the royal family, an attitude which he shares with Pentheus. For this reason he is punished along with the other family members.

Cadmus speaks for the ruling family; Teiresias speaks for god; we still have to hear the voice of the people. The men that Pentheus sent to arrest the Bacchant priest bring on Dionysus as a prisoner and their leader's short speech shows that he is conscious of the unusual and mystical in this new religion. Although at first only Teiresias and Cadmus were willing to acknowledge Dionysus, the men of Thebes show themselves ready to accept the implications of the amazing things they witness. The guard reports that the priest was not a wild animal ready to flee, as Pentheus had led them to believe, but was gentle, and calmly allowed them to tie his hands. The second unusual matter he reports is that the Bacchants whom Pentheus had earlier imprisoned are now free, and have gone to join the other women on the mountain. No human agency, he says, released the Bacchants from their bonds and from prison, and he immediately adds that the foreign priest has brought many wonders to Thebes and that Pentheus should now see to things. This man senses a connection between the miraculous events and the presence of the priest, but Pentheus ignores the implications of his words and proceeds to interrogate the prisoner according to his preconceived notions of what the cult involves. Although he has (as he thinks) their leader in his power, he asks for no explanation of the strange release of the Bacchants from prison, and enquires only about what he considers the cult's dissolute oriental practices. The ending of this scene resembles that with Teiresias, with Pentheus making violent threats, and his divine opponent warning about the king's blindness and lack of understanding. We can see that the god and the prophet share the same mind.

By the time Dionysus and Pentheus confront one another again there have been further miraculous happenings. After he has shattered the palace with an earthquake, Dionysus emerges once more and, acting as his own messenger, tells the chorus of his followers how a deluded Pentheus has struggled with a bull believing it to be Dionysus in his role as the foreign priest. When Pentheus actually appears he seems to be free of this god-induced delusion and as normal as we have seen him so far; that is, restless, excited and angry. Dionysus warns him to calm himself and pay attention to the man who is arriving with news of the women of Thebes and their activities on the mountain.

The messenger is a herdsman, an unsophisticated countryman, but he is a Theban citizen and, like Teiresias, gives a viewpoint, which is not that of the royal family. Dionysus draws attention to his arrival so that everyone knows who the man is and what he has come for, but the god also adds a warning specifically for Pentheus, "listen to his words and learn" (657). The herdsman says he "needs" to tell about the amazing doings of the Bacchant women on the mountain "to you and to the city", stressing the linkage that ideally should exist between the ruler and city. However, he first seeks reassurance that he can speak freely, since he knows that Pentheus is quick tempered and proud (666-71). It is not uncommon in Greek tragedy (or elsewhere) to find the humble messenger or soldier reluctant to give news that he realises will be unwelcome to his superior. Here, as in other plays, it is an expression of the tension between the aristocratic pride of a noble ruler and the commonsense will of the people for survival as a group. As the tragedies were intended to be played out with the Athenian democracy as their audience it is not surprising that this tension so often forms part of the dynamic of the dramas.

The vivid narrative of the events on the mountain not only paints a picture, but also carries a message for Pentheus if he cares to listen to it. When the herdsmen first sighted the women, who included Pentheus' mother Agave and his aunts, they were resting peacefully, not behaving immodestly, or drunk, as Pentheus had led them to believe. More amazingly, they enjoyed a wondrous communion with nature, suckling wild animals and able to produce wine, water and milk from the earth. Naturally the messenger associates these miraculous powers with the god and further asserts that if Pentheus had witnessed them he would pray to the god he now condemns (712). The idyllic scene on the mountain was disrupted as one of the herdsmen, a clever talker who had spent a lot time in the city, encouraged the others to try to catch Agave and so win favour from the king. When the attempt was made, the enraged women turned first on the herdsmen, who had to run away; they then attacked the herds, tearing apart the animals, tossing the mangled limbs on the ground. The women possessed more than human strength in their frenzy and ransacked the upland settlements and attacked any men who resisted, able to inflict wounds using only their bacchic *thyrsi*.

The messenger rounds off his report of the violent happenings by drawing the same conclusions and offering to Pentheus the same advice as after his more peaceful opening. The women's madness like their miracles must be of divine origin ("...not without some god", 764) and Pentheus should accept the new god into the city, because he is clearly powerful, but also because he gives men wine and hence the pleasures of love (!). The herdsman (man-in-the-street, or man-on-the-mountain) gives prominence to the same features of Dionysiac worship that Teiresias has already stressed, even though his account is less intellectually phrased. The power of the god is manifest in his miracles in the palace and in the powerful divine madness of the women on the mountain; human strength and weapons cannot withstand this power, as Teiresias warns and the Bacchants demonstrate. On the more domestic level, both prophet and herdsman stress the importance for men of the gift of wine and both try to make Pentheus look at the issue of sexual behaviour in a reasonable way. God and the people have spoken, with one voice.

As before, Pentheus reacts violently, ordering armed men to march against the Bacchants. He has rejected the advice of his subjects, in particular that of Teiresias and the herdsman; he now rejects completely Dionysus' final warning, which is, 'I say you should not take up arms against a god' (789). Pentheus' response ominously confirms his unwillingness to listen and learn, as he tells the god, 'Do not try to teach me' (792). There are no more warnings and, as the scene progresses, the young king is mentally invaded by the divine power so that he agrees to destroy his own identity as a male, as a ruler, and upholder of conventional religious practices. Thus he goes voluntarily to his death as a sacrificial victim for the god.

The scenes between Pentheus and the citizens of Thebes have obvious political implications. A ruler who loses touch with his subjects and refuses to listen to the voice of the people, can bring disaster to the whole state, and must be removed to ensure the continued life of the rest of the community. In *Bacchae*, Pentheus is destroyed and the royal family scattered, but the people remain to start again, presumably in a democratic way; 'The god accomplishes many things in unexpected ways.'

Bacchae:
the Revelation of Dionysus

David Raeburn

What makes an ancient Greek tragedy, composed for performance over 2400 years ago, still performable and exciting in the theatre today? The obvious answer must lie in a particular play's inherent quality as drama, that is its power to transcend its unfamiliar form and to re-engage an audience's emotional involvement in a rewarding experience. When it comes to *Bacchae*, one of the most powerful dramas ever written, we are bound also to respond to its universality. Though grounded in its own historical period and original conventions, it is a great play for all time, which has something to teach us about ourselves.

On the surface, it is a very odd play indeed. To summarise the plot in its barest essentials: Dionysus, the Greek god of wine and revelry, comes from the east to manifest his divinity in the city of Thebes where he was born, but where the sisters of his dead mother Semele have denied that he is the son of Zeus, king of the immortals. There he drives the women of the city mad and compels them to abandon their homes and families; the "maenads" flock together on Mount Cithaeron above Thebes, to lead a peculiar, back-to-nature kind of existence and perform strange rites in honour of the new god Dionysus, otherwise known as Bacchus. Violent opposition comes from Pentheus, the young king of Thebes, who regards the behaviour of his mother Agavë and the other bacchanals as an obscenity, which he is determined to root out. The main action of the play shows the god himself, in the guise of a very attractive mortal (he poses as a male devotee of the god and leads the Chorus of bacchanals who have accompanied him in a revel-band from Asia), confronting Pentheus and gradually getting him into his own power. Pentheus is eventually induced by Dionysus to go up to the mountain dressed as a bacchanal to spy on the maenads, who frenziedly tear his body to pieces in the belief that he is a "climbing animal". The closing episode shows Agavë on stage, triumphantly bearing her son's head, which she thinks is a lion's, then coming back to her senses and being faced with the frightful horror of what she has done. So Dionysus manifests his divinity – in a particularly cruel, gruesome and bizarre kind of way. What are we to make of this play, which we may note that Euripides composed towards the very end of his life on a visit to Macedonia, to the mountainous north of Greece, and which was only performed at Athens after he had died?

Let us first explore a little of what Dionysus meant in Greek religion. He was one of the twelve Olympians, though more of a god of confusion than of order in the universe. His cult was widely established throughout Greece, but was of a more exotic character than many others; for example, the sacrifices to him might involve the dedication and consumption of raw meat, instead of meat which was roasted or boiled. But much of the detail in *Bacchae* itself must be based on the god's mystery cult at Athens, which included a feature of transvestism in its initiation rituals. Among his other attributes, he was the god of festivals at which tragedies and comedies were presented, extremely important events in the life of the Athenian community. Quite exceptionally, *Bacchae* is a play based on a myth about Dionysus himself.

The Greek tragedians nearly always based their plays on inherited stories or myths about the gods and/or human characters derived from the heroic world. They were free to treat these myths in their own way, very much in accordance with their own vision of human affairs and man's relationship with the universe. We thus find the three great tragic poets – Aeschylus, Sophocles and Euripides – giving quite different dramatic treatments to the story of Orestes' murder of his mother Clytemnestra, in revenge for the killing of his father Agamemnon. The god Apollo, who gives Orestes his instructions, emerges differently in each of the three plays. Euripides, indeed, is critical of Apollo in his *Electra*, which emphasises Orestes' matricide not as a just revenge but as a peculiarly revolting crime. He seems to raise the question: is a god who actually tells a man to *kill his own mother* a god whom the Greeks really ought to worship? Euripides was part of the "intellectual revolution" which affected Athens, under the influence of teachers known as Sophists, during the latter part of the 5th century B.C.E., when traditionally held views of the gods and morality were being questioned. The most interesting question, to my mind, raised by *Bacchae* is the following: in dramatizing the manifestation of Dionysus, how is Euripides himself manifesting the god of the dramatic festivals? If there is a critique, it looks a very bold one, which the poet might well have reserved for the end of his life, when he was away from Athens amid the mountains of Macedonia.

We need first to consider how Euripides seems to regard Dionysus as a force in human life. We may compare his treatment of Aphrodite, the goddess of sex, in another of his greatest tragedies, *Hippolytus*. In that play Aphrodite is clearly presented as an essential element in the universe: "she moves in the air and is found in the sea-waves, and all things owe their being. She is the one who sows and bestows desire, from which all of us on earth are sprung." The drama portrays the puritanically virginal Hippolytus rejecting Aphrodite and being cruelly destroyed for it. The message may be that no one can safely afford to repress their sexual instincts. Thus Pentheus' disastrous opposition to Dionysus in *Bacchae* might be thought to contain a similar warning against fighting a fundamental force in human nature. However, when one looks at the text closely, Euripides is evidently approaching Dionysus in a much more complex and subtle way.

It is clear that the god is (for him) a lot more than simply the god of wine, though that is a starting-off point. One of Dionysus' cult-titles was Lyaeus, Releaser, which fairly obviously derives from the power of wine to loosen people's inhibitions and encourage them to abandon restraint, treat life as it comes and allow untrammelled emotion its head. But Dionysus is essentially worshipped in groups; so he also represents an instinct to follow the herd, "get with it" and be swept up in a tide of crowd emotion. It is these, more far-reaching, aspects of Dionysus that Euripides seems to be exploring in *Bacchae*, if we carefully analyse the words and behaviour of his individual characters and, most importantly, in the poetry which is given to the Chorus to sing.

Consider first of all Euripides' portrayal of the god himself. At the end of the scene in which Pentheus clearly surrenders to his spell, Dionysus describes himself as "a god of terror and a god of gentle comfort for mankind". There is an obvious paradox here in a god who is both fearsome and mild. His physical appearance initially and for most of the play supports the "mild" interpretation. In his mortal disguise, he actually has a sensuously feminine look, with long, soft curly hair and a perpetual smile shown on his mask. His behaviour in the scenes with Pentheus is generally relaxed and cool ("cool" even in the sophisticated modern sense), and his calmness contrasts with Pentheus' restless excitability. When the god is brought in chains before his opponent for interrogation, we have no doubt that he is quietly in control of the whole situation; similarly when he walks out of prison unscathed, and later when he seduces Pentheus with his invitation to spy on the bacchanals. At the end of that episode he gloatingly speaks to the Chorus about revenge on Pentheus in a more sinister tone; but he subsequently returns to gentle mockery in the macabre transvestite scene, where Pentheus returns attired in all the bacchic gear before going off to his horrible death on the mountain. Only after Pentheus has made his final exit is the god terrifying in his triumph. Very shortly afterwards the Chorus calls on Dionysus to manifest himself in one of his animal forms – as a bull, snake or lion. So when the god appears again in a formal epiphany on the roof of the stage building in the closing scene, we can imagine him dressed in formidable magnificence and wearing a mask which portrays his relentless cruelty, perhaps with animal features such as the bull's horns which Pentheus in his intoxicated condition has seen on him. The perpetual smile on Dionysus' earlier mask can now be remembered as "the smile on the face of the tiger".

The lyrics which Euripides puts in the mouths of his Chorus of Asiatic bacchanals are revealing in a more elaborate way. In their entrance-song the women express the rapturous joy and beauty of the bacchic cult; and their dance reaches an ecstatic climax in an extraordinary description of a mountain revel of screaming women, led by a long-haired male figure representing the god himself, to the banging accompaniment of the drum and the lotus-reed pipe. It all sounds as harmless as a contemporary pop-festival, although there are a couple of sinister hints in the violent potential of the thyrsus, the ivy-clad wand which all the bacchanals carry, and in the "joy of eating raw flesh". In their second song, the chorus responds with indignation to Pentheus' planned arrest of the young stranger who represents Dionysus for them; but their song as a whole is in a sensuous, relaxed rhythm and celebrates Dionysus as a healer of human cares, who sends men to sleep through the power of wine. In this poem we are also given a glimpse of the intellectual attitude which Dionysus exemplifies: "clever is not wise" and "the common way that's best for all is best for me". Euripides here makes his bacchanals identify with the values of the man-in-the-street – in modern terms, with the viewpoint of the tabloids rather than the broadsheet press. This is confirmed by their escape-prayer, "I wish I were in Cyprus now, the land of love and Aphrodite, land of lust and longing, sweet seduction of soft eyes" (*Hello* magazine?).

In their third poem, the chorus deplores their rejection by Thebes and vents their hatred on Pentheus, the "mud-man, born of the dragon's blood" – the imagery is growing more earthy and bestial. They go on to invoke Dionysus, "urging his hunting pack" on the mountain heights of northern Greece. Their next song, as the god's punishment of Pentheus draws closer, is even more menacing. In a repeated refrain they define the "wisdom" they prefer to "cleverness": it is simply the "power to overcome our enemies, to bring our hands down heavy on their heads". So the wisdom of the bacchanals is equated with brutal vindictiveness! Their final words extol a levelling of ambition and a philosophy which "lives from day to day". No wonder, then, that after Pentheus has left for the mountain dressed in women's clothes, the Chorus launches into a frenetic irregular rhythm, to call furiously on the dogs of Madness to possess Pentheus' mother and the other Theban women who are going to tear him to pieces; the climax of the song is an impassioned invocation of Bacchus to appear in his various animal manifestations.

Thus Euripides employs one of Greek tragedy's two root elements, the Chorus, to reveal both the joy and the terror which Dionysus stands for. He also uses his other basic convention, the Messenger Speech, to very telling effect. In fact, he gives us two Messenger narrations, both recounting the behaviour of the Theban bacchanals as they carry out their strange rites on the slopes of Mount Cithaeron. The first is delivered by a simple Herdsman: the women who have left their homes and children are behaving perfectly peacefully in tune with nature, which is miraculously supplying their physical needs, while they tie their deerskin dresses with coils of serpents or suckle fawns and wolf-cubs in their arms. Tranquillity is disrupted when a colleague herdsman suggests that the men present should ambush the women and bring Agavë back as a prisoner to her son Pentheus. As the maenads are disturbed during a trance-like dance, they suddenly run wild. The hunted then become the hunters, and the herdsmen flee. But the women start attacking the cattle instead of the herdsmen, and tear them to pieces; after which they descend to the villages in the valley below and ransack everything they can find, miraculously routing the men who come out to attack them, before returning to their activities on the mountain. This account foreshadows the second, even more powerful, Messenger speech, which describes Pentheus' observation of the Theban bacchanals in their peaceful state from the top of a pine-tree. Suddenly they are disturbed once again by a loud voice from heaven calling on them to punish the intruder who has mocked their mysteries. The reaction is violence once again: with superhuman strength the women uproot Pentheus' pine-tree, so that he falls to the ground, there to be set on and ripped to pieces by his demented mother and her sisters. Both these great Messenger speeches, therefore, are used by Euripides to demonstrate first the tranquillity and then the mindless violence of Dionysus in action; the two moods are shown to be reverse sides of the same coin.

What of the older generations among the characters? Pentheus' old grandfather, the former King Cadmus, and the aged seer Teiresias are shown early on in the play ludicrously dressed up as bacchanals, their dignity forgotten, tagging on to the new cult – but not because Dionysus has driven them mad like the Theban women. Cadmus is willing to join in because, if Dionysus was Semele's son by Zeus, it is prestigious to have a god in the family. Teiresias, as the prophet of Apollo, represents conventional Greek religion coming to terms with the more exotic and ecstatic elements of the Dionysiac cult, by attempting to rationalize its more outrageous features. (Historically, Dionysus was allowed to preside at Delphi in classical times during the winter months when Apollo's oracle was closed.) Dionysus evidently attracts a certain amount of humbug into the bargain! This scene contains an obvious element of satire, and its positioning after the Chorus's entrance-song provides an interesting perspective both on that and all the rest of the play.

As for Pentheus' mother, Agavë, who has led her fellow-bacchanals in the king's appalling destruction and in "playing ball" with pieces of his flesh, I know of no more horrifying moment in drama than the point where her madness leaves her and she suddenly realizes that the severed head she is cradling in her arms is not the head of a lion, but of her own son. After that, she can only follow her father Cadmus in bemoaning Dionysus' cruelty; she wants nothing more to do with the rites she has so ardently practised.

I have left Pentheus till last as he is in some ways the most interestingly delineated character in the whole play. In his opposition to Dionysus he paradoxically exposes Dionysus' nature as tellingly as all the others. Pentheus is not portrayed as the voice of cool reason or social order protesting against the emotional character of the bacchic cult and its disruptive effect on the normal activities of women. On the contrary, he fights Dionysus quite irrationally, that is with the Dionysus in himself. It is clear from his first entrance that he is an extremely excitable person, whose fury with the bacchanals and the Lydian stranger who has infected them is based more on his imagination than on fact. He envisages the Theban women indulging in drunken orgies and going off one by one into the bushes to serve the lusts of men. (When we hear from the first Messenger what the bacchanals are actually doing on the mountainside, it is clear that they are not getting drunk or having sex with men behind bushes.) Later, when a soldier brings the arrested Dionysus before Pentheus, the first meeting between the two is quite extraordinary. Pentheus is so fascinated by the stranger's physical beauty, that he appears not to hear the soldier's report that some bacchae whom the king has imprisoned have miraculously escaped and returned to their rites. The obsession with sex seems to run through his interrogation of Dionysus, which leaves us in the end with the impression of a hot-tempered, repressed, insecure young man who relies on bluster to assert his authority. The impression is reinforced when Dionysus escapes from the prison where Pentheus has tried to incarcerate him and describes the teasing of the king with the phantom of a bull, which Pentheus frantically tries to bind in chains, believing the beast to be the god. (It is not difficult to understand this as Pentheus vainly fighting against the animal – the Dionysus – in himself.) All this makes the turning-point completely credible, when the god finally counters the king's threats against the bacchae by asking: "Do you want to see them for yourself – up there on the mountainside?" and is given the breathy reply, "Yes! Yes I do! I'd give a lot to see that!" Pentheus has now ultimately responded to what was there inside him all the time. He himself exhibits Dionysus operating in the individual (as distinct from the group) as the personification of untrammelled emotion; and this is the ultimate subtlety in what is an intellectually challenging, as well as a deeply exciting and moving, drama.

Bacchae has particularly attracted directors for performance in the modern theatre. For one thing, the Chorus with its vigorous movement and dancing offers scope for the more athletic, as opposed to declamatory, approach to classical drama that has won favour in recent decades. For another, the psychology of Pentheus seems peculiarly modern; and there are general parallels to be drawn with the pop-music scene and even the drug culture. The Dionysiac ethos seems more appealing than dangerous, and some may want to explain Pentheus' awful demise as a warning that the Dionysus in oneself should not be resisted, even if it can find expression in rabid fanaticism backed by obsession with sex. But such an interpretation rests on a misconception. The central figure in Bacchae is not Pentheus, but Dionysus. If we look at the shape and tendency of the play as it develops towards its horrific climax, we see that the main theme must be Dionysus himself in all his different aspects. One important feature is the steady growth in Euripides' use of imagery drawn from the world of animals and hunting. Another is the frequent use of words denoting "manifestation", "seeing" and "understanding" throughout the Greek text. As Dionysus reveals himself, so Euripides is gradually revealing Dionysus and what he represents. The exposé is summed up in the gentleness/terror paradox. Beguiling and beautiful as it may be to give free rein to emotion, to abandon our critical faculties and "get with it", this is to blur the distinction between human and animal, indeed to make ourselves more like animals and less like human beings. This, surely, is the moral message.

Euripides will have seen much that was Dionysiac in the history of his own time. The last three decades of his life were dominated by the war between Athens and Sparta, which we can learn about in Thucydides' Histories. It is clear from this great book that the Athenian democracy, for all its cultural achievements, suffered from an instability and proneness to violence which contributed to its eventual defeat. Euripides must have been acutely aware of the dangers of popular decision-making – though Bacchae is not making a political statement so much as a comment on human nature and the mentality of the crowd.

How do we encounter Dionysus is our own world? I have already suggested that he may be found in the relentlessly throbbing music of the pop-festival, or in the pages of the sensational tabloids whose aim is to feed their readers what they want at a basic instinctive level rather than to invite them to think. Another often-quoted example is the phenomenon of crowds manipulated by demagogues with vicious hatred against a minority, as Hitler orchestrated feelings against the Jews in 1930's Germany. Everyone knows how crowd behaviour at a football match can suddenly turn nasty and result in violent behaviour. To take an even more commonplace situation, many teenagers have found themselves involved, against their will and better natures, in the persecution of an ineffective classroom teacher; it starts with the insolence of one or two, then spreads until the cruelty pervades the whole group in a way which individuals afterwards find inexplicable and deplorable. The extraordinary surge of popular feeling which followed the death of Princess Diana was another Dionysiac occasion in the eyes of those who did not see it as an unusual mark of national solidarity (such as at the funeral of the late Queen Mother) so much as the collective indulgence of hysterical emotion. However we interpret that, Dionysus is with us as much as Aphrodite, and we need to "take precautions" against his ill effects by critical thinking and self-control.

If *Bacchae*, regarded in universal terms, serves as a warning against untrammelled emotion, is its tragic conclusion entirely pessimistic? I end with a more careful look at the play's closing scene, which is difficult to reconstruct as quite a large number of lines have disappeared from the original Greek text. As Agavë holds Pentheus' head in her arms, her father

Cadmus has entered, bearing the dismembered parts of Pentheus' body on some sort of bier. The missing lines almost certainly included a lament by Agavë over her son's body, during which she arranges the severed limbs in an orderly way and finally returns the head to its proper position. This reassembling of the corpse might perhaps be viewed, symbolically, as a gesture of reintegration after the havoc caused by the violent forces of nature which Dionysus represents. People today do cope with violent death by orderly funerals and other mourning rituals. Public grief for those who die in war, sectarian murders or acts of individual savagery may be assuaged to a degree, as at the death of Princess Diana, by the simple action of laying flowers. So tragedies in the theatre may be shatteringly depressing in their emotional impact; but the greatest sometimes offer a glimpse of light by introducing some note of consolation or, at least, a sense of order restored. So, maybe, with Euripides' *Bacchae*.

Note: Most of the ideas in this essay have been drawn from the late Professor R.P. Winnington-Ingram's scholarly and thoughtful interpretation of Bacchae in *Euripides and Dionysus*, first published by the Cambridge University Press in 1948 and lately reissued. This book is strongly recommended to any who wish to study the play further.

What Ought the Thebans to Have Done?

Alan H. Sommerstein

Something goes terribly wrong in *Bacchae*. The god Dionysus, son of the Theban princess Semele, has returned to Thebes to establish his cult there. Every spectator watching the play at the City Dionysia knows that this cult, like Dionysus' gift of wine, can bring great pleasure and great release of mental tension. And yet its arrival in Thebes produces catastrophe. Semele's nephew Pentheus, the king of Thebes, is torn in pieces by his mother Agaue, her sisters Ino and Autonoe, and the other women of Thebes; Agaue returns to Thebes in triumph, believing she has killed a lion, and displaying Pentheus' head on the end of her ritual rod (*thyrsos*); and finally the entire family, including Agaue's aged father Cadmus, are expelled from the city. Why has this happened?

In one sense, Dionysus himself answers this question right at the beginning. Semele, made pregnant by Zeus, had perished through the guile of Zeus's ever-jealous consort Hera. The story (told somewhat allusively in *Bacchae*) is that Hera, in disguise, persuaded Semele to ask Zeus to visit her in his full divine splendour; Zeus, having promised Semele to do whatever she wished, could not refuse her request, and the lightning-fire of his presence destroyed her. Zeus snatched her unborn infant from the flames and sewed him up in his own thigh, eventually to be "born" a second time.

Cadmus turned Semele's house and tomb into a

shrine (6-12). Her sisters Agaue, Ino and Autonoe took a very different view (26-31). They claimed that Semele had really been pregnant by a mortal lover, and at her father's suggestion had covered her shame by pretending Zeus was the father of her baby, and that Zeus had destroyed her to punish this lie. Because of this slander, the three sisters, with all the other women of Thebes, have been "driven in madness from their homes", and made to wear Dionysus' sacred garb and perform his rituals (32-38).

That, however, need not have had catastrophic results. If Thebes, as Dionysus puts it (39-40), "learn[s] … that it is uninitiated in my bacchic cult", and adopts it officially, Dionysus will doubtless let the women go home (cf. 804-7). But will Thebes do that? Not if Pentheus has his way. He "fights against the gods," says Dionysus, "or at least against me, debars me from libations, and does not mention me in his prayers" (45-46); he may try to bring the women home by force – in which case Dionysus will "join with the maenads as their general" (52) with unstated, but evidently fatal, results for Pentheus.

Dionysus' indictment of Pentheus may at first sight seem a little unjust. Pentheus was abroad when Dionysus came to Thebes (215), and has had no way of knowing that he even exists, much less that he demands universal worship. What is more, it is perfectly reasonable that he should believe Semele's infant had perished (since that is what normally happens when a pregnant woman suffers a violent death, and no one in Greece knows of any evidence to the contrary) and perfectly reasonable that he should believe the baby's father was not Zeus (for Zeus would not have destroyed his own offspring). But whatever sympathy we may initially have for him is dissipated with extraordinary rapidity as we get to know him better. Dionysus' condemnation is quite unjustified in terms of what Pentheus had done *previously*; but what Pentheus does *subsequently* shows, at the very least, that he was riding for a fall of some sort.

Pentheus starts putting himself in the wrong almost from the moment he appears. He has imprisoned numerous free-born women in chains (226-232) on the basis of unsubstantiated rumour ("I hear" 216, "they say" 233). If he catches their priest (who is really Dionysus in disguise) he will execute him by stoning (356) or by decapitation (241) – a punishment utterly abhorrent to Greeks – and there is no indication that there will be any trial. He tells his own grandfather that he is making a ridiculous fool of himself (250-2, 344-5). He accuses the prophet Teiresias of being complicit in the introduction of the new cult in the hope of increasing his professional income (255-7) – and we know that when someone accuses Teiresias of corruption it is always a bad sign (ask Oedipus, or Creon in *Antigone*); later he orders the physical destruction of Teiresias' seat of augury (346-351), thus putting himself in the wrong with Apollo as well as Dionysus. No wonder Teiresias ends the scene (367-9) by hoping that Pentheus, whose name means "man of grief", may not bring grief to Cadmus and his family.

So far, as we have seen, Pentheus has spoken and acted entirely on the basis of rumour – some of which will prove completely false (notably the allegation that the women's bacchic rites are a cover for sexual debauchery). Now he begins to receive authentic information, which makes it obvious that a god is at work. The guard who has arrested the supposed priest reports that the imprisoned women have been miraculously liberated, their feet being unchained, and the prison doors opened, by no mortal hand (443-8): Pentheus' response, incredibly, is to order the guards to let go of the priest's arms, "because now he is in the net, he is not speedy enough to escape me" (451-2). It is as if he had not heard what had just been said to him – not the last instance of such selective deafness or blindness. And after an interview in which contempt of the new cult is strangely mingled with curiosity (cf. 471-480), he has the "priest" locked up in the palace stables, and gratuitously adds that his Asian followers will be seized as slaves (511-4).

There follows another miracle, or series of miracles, of which this time Pentheus is an eyewitness. A mighty voice is heard; the palace shakes; the sacred fire on Semele's tomb suddenly flares up; and presently the "priest" walks calmly out of the palace, his prison having been demolished. Pentheus meanwhile has been kept busy tying up a bull (618-621), fighting the fire, and trying to kill a phantom (629-631). Surely by now he must have some suspicion that he is up against something too powerful for him? Not in the least: his next order is to close all the city's gates (653) as if this were a routine jailbreak.

The final proof that Pentheus' whole approach is both false and dangerous comes immediately afterwards, as a herdsman arrives with news from Mount Cithaeron. He has seen the bacchants on the mountain, and they are as orderly as a military garrison. They are divided into three companies, each under a commander (680-2), they rise promptly at reveille (689-694) and adjust their uniforms carefully (695-8), they perform their rituals at fixed times (723-4), and sexuality and drunkenness are nowhere to be detected. On the other hand, the impossible and the miraculous seem to be matters of routine: the women use live snakes as belts (698), suckle fawns and wolf-cubs (699-702), and by a stroke or a touch make the ground flow with milk, honey, water and wine (704-711). All utterly amazing, and utterly unthreatening – except of course that society will collapse if the women aren't restored to sanity, and to Thebes, fairly soon. This, though, cannot be done by force, as the rest of the herdsman's narrative makes clear. When he and his friends, encouraged by a know-all from the city (717-721), try to capture the women, they immediately run amok, tear cattle in pieces, raid two villages and put the armed inhabitants to flight; and loads do not burden them, fire does not burn them, weapons do not wound them. How will Pentheus respond to this?

He responds in his accustomed manner. He has by now witnessed, or been credibly informed of, fifteen or twenty manifest miracles. And as ever, he neither accepts nor denies their reality; he just ignores them. He orders an immediate military expedition against the bacchants (780-5), vowing to "stir up a great deal of women's blood" on Mount Cithaeron (796-7) – oblivious, it seems, to the fact, of which we have recently been repeatedly reminded (682, 690, 720, 728), that one of these women is his own mother. It is perhaps significant that he refers to them as his "slaves" (803), as if he were the King of Persia –doubly ironic, this, considering how he prides himself on his Greekness (483, 779) in contrast to barbarians like the Lydian "priest" and his followers. We now expect the threatened military expedition (cf. 52) to be launched, and Dionysus to take command of his maenad army as promised. What happens is rather different.

For at this moment Dionysus shows that he is, after all, a god of justice. Pentheus has shown himself a tyrant with no respect for man or god, ready to insult his grandfather, imprison or kill his mother, chop off heads on mere suspicion, and treat free people like slaves, wilfully blind and deaf to the plainest evidence that a superhuman agency is at work – and yet Dionysus offers him a way out. "I will bring the women here," he says, "without the use of arms" (804). Thebes can be restored to normality without any blood being shed. Of course, there is a price: the definitive establishment of Dionysiac cult at Thebes (807-8). But why on earth not? On all the available evidence, the cult brings pleasure and, unless provoked, no pain. But Pentheus will have none of it: "Bring me my armour out here. And you, stop talking." (809)

The disguised god doesn't stop talking, and Pentheus never gets his armour; in fact, the next time we see him he will be dressed as a woman, and the time after that he will be a set of detached body parts.

Pentheus' approach to the Dionysiac phenomenon has been a disastrous failure, and this naturally leads us to ask what alternative approach, if any, could have been successful. The play actually offers us a considerable range of options, before it narrows its focus to show us the consequences of the one chosen by Pentheus.

The first of these options is presented by the chorus of Lydian bacchants in their opening song (parodos). One part of this song narrates the birth(s) and infancy of Dionysus; other parts give a detailed and evocative picture of his ecstatic worship, first in the streets (64-87), then in the mountains (135-169). The song is full of "barbarian" elements: the women are Asian, they wear the weird garb of bacchic ritual, carry and doubtless beat drums; there are repeated references to Lydia, Phrygia, even Syria, all of which to the Greek mind were places that slaves came from. The mountain ritual consists of running, leaping, falling, dancing, singing, shouting, with drums, pipes and torches, and its focus and object is to hunt down goats, tear them in pieces and eat their raw flesh (139). It may well be doubted how anyone could think it wise to introduce such practices as this into a society that wished to be sane and safe. In particular, a crucial psychological prerequisite, apparently, is what the chorus call "communalizing the soul" (75-76): abandoning individuality, merging one's personality in the swarm. Such an experience can be extremely uplifting and pleasurable. It can also, however, be extremely dangerous: "herd instinct", "crowd hysteria", "mob violence", are all designations of what can happen if this process gets out of hand. The Greek *polis* is a place where law rules and where the individual citizen is responsible for his actions. At the very least, even if one accepts that a degree of uninhibited release may be beneficial, it must be kept within some kind of boundaries. There is no sign that this chorus is willing to accept anything of the kind. They claim authority over the streets and houses and their inhabitants (68-70); they become animalized, wearing fawnskins and galloping like fillies (137-8, 164-9); they tear animals apart as if they owned them, not caring that goats might have a goatherd. If this is what Thebes and Pentheus are being offered, one can well understand if they feel they have to reject it.

Next we see two Thebans, Teiresias and Cadmus, both aged men. They may not be able to gallop like fillies or tear goats in pieces, but they do believe it is their duty to join in the worship of Dionysus. They have, though, two very different approaches to the cult.

The fate of Cadmus in the play may well seem unjust. Early in the prologue Dionysus praises Cadmus for creating a shrine to Semele (10-11), and we learn also that he, unlike his daughters, had always publicly maintained that Semele's lover had been none other than Zeus. On learning that Semele's son has returned to Thebes as a god, Cadmus is eager to do him honour. That Cadmus is in the end bereaved of his treasured grandson is of course not inconsistent with this: the punishment of the guilty inevitably has side-effects on their innocent kin. But Cadmus also receives from Dionysus a specific punishment of his own: exile from Thebes to a barbarian land, and transformation into a snake (1330-4, 1354-60). It is true that he will eventually go to the Isles of the Blest (1337-8), but overall his fate is undoubtedly meant as a punishment, as Dionysus makes clear in words that are addressed to Cadmus as well as his daughters:

> If you had known to be sensible, when you refused to be, you would now be happy, with the son of Zeus for your ally. ... You have understood us too late; you did not know us when you should have done. ... I was a god, and you insulted me. (1341-7)

And Cadmus admits the charge (1344, 1346, 1377-8), even while pleading for mercy. What is he admitting being guilty of? If the play offers an explanation at all (and surely it ought to), it must come in the scene in which Cadmus and Teiresias are confronted by Pentheus. It may not matter much that Cadmus tells Pentheus that "even if, as you claim, this god does not exist, *you* should pretend he does" for the honour of Semele and the family (333-6); taken by itself, that might be just Cadmus desperately trying to get through to Pentheus with an argument that might possibly appeal to him. But Cadmus had spoken like that to Teiresias too:

> I have come prepared, wearing this sacred attire of the god;
> for since he is my daughter's son, it is right
> that he should be magnified and glorified to the best of our ability. (180-3)

Admittedly Cadmus, as the first mortal ever to have a god for a grandchild, is in a unique position with no precedent to guide him, but his language strongly suggests that he is magnifying and glorifying Dionysus *only* because Dionysus is his grandson – doing, in fact, precisely what he later recommends Pentheus to do, and "telling a fine lie" in the family's interest. His attitude also changes the significance of what we heard in the prologue: the insistence that Semele's lover had been divine, the creation of a shrine to her, now look like the contrivances of a head of family determined to put a positive spin on what might have been a very shaming episode. To say the least, we cannot be sure he actually believes Dionysus is a god.

Now it is true that Greek religion, generally speaking, was a matter of practice rather than of belief. The gods, on the whole, didn't mind what mortals thought about them, so long as they received their dues in the form of prayer and especially sacrifice. But as the trial of Socrates would soon show, belief couldn't be ignored, because it could have an effect on practice. If the belief spreads that the gods do not really exist, sooner or later the community will decide that it can use its resources better than by sending them up in smoke to these non-existent gods – and if by any chance the gods do in fact exist, such a decision could have unfortunate consequences. And Dionysus, in particular, can only be truly worshipped by those who throw their whole being into the act of worship – and one can hardly be doing that if one is thinking of Dionysus as a family asset. It is therefore appropriate that whereas the chorus of Asian devotees condemns Pentheus (263-5) and praises Teiresias (328-9), they say nothing at all about Cadmus.

Teiresias, in tragedy, is nearly always right, and the audience may well look to him for some words of pious wisdom in an attempt to set Pentheus on a more prudent path. They may perhaps be disappointed. Teiresias speaks less like a prophet than like a sophist. He rationalizes everything; all the mystery and the ecstasy disappear. Dionysus is the inventor of (or perhaps *is*) wine, which is good for drowning sorrows, inducing sleep, and pouring in libations. He was never sewn up in Zeus's thigh; that story was created through the confusion of two similar-sounding words. He also has (in reality rather minor) connections with prophecy and war. And while Dionysus will not compel women to be chaste, a woman who *is* truly chaste by nature will not change her nature under his influence (which, for an overwhelmingly male audience that was not disposed to think particularly highly of women's moral capacity, would beg a very big question). All this is all very well, but it has little to do with the kind of ecstatic worship that we have heard partly described, partly enacted by the chorus in their opening lyric. It is an attempt to tame Dionysus and make him into a reasonable god that reasonable, educated late fifth-century Athenians can rationally worship. If that is the kind of god he wants to be, he would never have come to Thebes accompanied by these outlandish barbarian women.

Or so we probably think, until the scene ends and the outlandish barbarian women sing their second ode. And to our surprise we find that all the wild ecstasies have vanished, to be replaced by the not exactly sober, but at any rate bounded and socialized pleasures of that civilized, urban(e) institution, the symposium (376-385). The chorus commend "a life of quietness and good sense" (389-390) and warn against the danger of "not thinking mortal thoughts" and of "chasing great things" instead of making the best of what one can get (395-9). They pray to be taken to Cyprus or Pieria (402-416), the lands of Aphrodite and of the Muses. The connection between Dionysus and the Muses would be obvious to every Athenian spectator; and Aphrodite, as the Herdsman will remind us (773-4), is (in the right context) an essential part of the good life. In the final stanza Dionysus' association with "the painless delight of wine" is re-emphasized, as is his democratic nature: he offers his gifts "equally to the prosperous and the inferior" (421-2). More than once the chorus express a rejection of what may be called intellectualism (*to sophon*, 395); true intelligence (*sophia*) is something different – it is accepting the human condition and the opinions and practices of "the masses of ordinary people" (430). This distinction between two contrasting connotations of *sophia* – being clever enough to know what's good for one, and being too clever for one's own good – runs right through the play.

42

Is this the answer we have been seeking? It seems surprisingly banal and naïve, and resolutely oblivious to the tragic aspects of human existence. Accept life's pleasures – song, dance, food, drink, sex, sleep, and good company (the listing is Kenneth Dover's – in another, though still Dionysiac, context – and all of them figure in the choral ode we have been looking at); don't try to rationalize them into conformity with some high-flown philosophical schema; respect popular traditions, especially religious ones; that is true wisdom, and will bring happiness. Naïve or not, this view does seem to be endorsed by all the Theban *commoners* we see in the play. The guard who arrested the disguised god was reluctant to do so and told his prisoner as much (441-2), and he tells Pentheus "this man … is full of miracles" (449-450). The herdsman, though fearful of the king's anger (670-1), urges him to accept the new god, not least because "they say … he gave mortals the vine which puts a stop to grief; and if there is no more wine, there is no more Aphrodite, nor any other human pleasure" (771-4). And the messenger who reports Pentheus' death concludes that "to know one's place (*sophronein*) and revere the divine is best, and I think it is also wisest" (1150-1).

There is, after all, no contradiction in believing that life has both its tragedies, many of them unavoidable, and its pleasures, and that since total renunciation of the pleasures will not help one escape the tragedies, it is foolish not to accept them (within reason, of course). If Pentheus has rejected normal pleasures (and one certainly doubts if he'd make a good companion for a symposium), it seems only to have led him to seek perverted ones: his way of showing affection for his grandfather had been to ask whom Cadmus wanted him to punish (1310-2, 1318-22), and he is lured to his death by being offered the chance to spy on the maenads' alleged sexual orgies. And his evidence-proof hatred and contempt for Dionysus and all he stands for leads to an appalling catastrophe that was entirely avoidable.

It remains true that though Pentheus and Cadmus, Agaue and Ino and Autonoe, have all deserved to suffer, they all suffer far more than they deserve, or than anyone deserves – and *that* is the note on which the play ends. It may well be, as Richard Seaford supposes, that Dionysus' speech as *deus ex machina* (most of which has been lost from the only manuscript) included instructions for establishing an organized cult of Dionysus at Thebes; but the Thebans who will benefit from that cult are not on stage. Those who are present are Cadmus, the lonely old man facing a future he loathes; Agaue, the mother who has killed her son; and that son's dismembered body, over whose torn limbs, one by one, Agaue, in another lost passage, had lovingly lamented. As often in Euripides, human love seems the only consolation in a cruel world: father and daughter part with an embrace (1363-7), and Agaue will share her exile with her sisters (1381-2). They themselves may have made the world crueller than it need have been, but we can pity them nevertheless – as even the chorus do (1327-8).

And we can go a little beyond pity. In the play's last genuine words, Agaue says:

May I go where
foul Cithaeron shall never see me again
nor I set eyes on Cithaeron,
and where no *thyrsos* is dedicated, to remind me!

Let them be the concern of *other* bacchants!
(1383-7)

Just as the savage zeal of Pentheus was counter-
productive, so too, at least in one respect, has been
the zealous savagery of his cousin Dionysus. It has
benefited nobody, at least in Thebes (since Dionysus
could have destroyed Pentheus, or rendered him
harmless, in many less atrocious ways), and it has
irrevocably alienated this sister of Semele. It is
entirely understandable that Agaue should thus
loathe and shun that which caused her ruin. She
cannot be expected to reflect – but we should – that
so many things in this world have caused the ruin of
someone at some time that we cannot possibly shun
them all. We have seen in this play that Dionysus is
a risky, destabilizing god; but deliberately,
obsessively to avoid all risk and instability is itself
risky and destabilizing. And deliberately, obsessively
to avoid pleasure as such merely ensures that life will
be all pain – as if there wasn't enough of that anyway.

Individualism, the Community and the Lost Words of Dionysus

Richard Seaford

A fundamental tension in the *Bacchae* is between on the one hand the chorus, who are prepared to merge their souls in a single body, the *thiasos* (75), and on the other the stubborn, impermeable individualism of Pentheus.

One element in Pentheus' individualism is - I have only recently come to realise - seeing pleasure in terms of money: that is the significance of the (otherwise rather curious) response he makes to Dionysos' question whether he would like to see the maenads sitting together on the mountainside (811). Here, at the turning point of the play, he says "yes indeed, and I would give a huge weight of gold (to do so)". This contrasts with the subsequent choral song, in which the chorus state that what we would call the rat-race, the insecure struggle for wealth and power, is inferior to the lasting joy brought by Dionysiac initiation to the here and now (if, unlike most translators, we understand aright lines 857-912). The Greek *polis* was the first society in history to be thoroughly monetised, and Dionysiac cult is older than this monetisation.

Monetisation is only one factor in the impermeable individualism of Pentheus. Another is the isolation of the mystic initiand, which has (along with various other experiences of the initiand) been projected onto the sufferings and curious behaviour of Pentheus. The struggle between individual and collective is finally decided in favour of the latter. Mystic experience should be, as the chorus itself make clear

(72-5), collective, and is sometimes embodied at the centre of a collective festival of the *polis*.

This eventual victory of the collective over the individual is often obscured by the curious but widespread idea that the outcome of the play is disaster for Thebes. There is not a word to suggest this. Why do critics assume that in the *Bacchae* the destruction of the Theban monarchy, which is described as a tyranny, is a disaster rather than a blessing for Thebes? Does this blindness arise from their emotional investment in the British monarchy, whose violent destruction would undoubtedly be presented as national disaster?

In fact the destruction (or self-destruction) of the Theban royal family is, however pitiful, no disaster for Thebes. Quite the reverse: there is much (including the words of Dionysos himself in the prologue) to suggest that at the end of the play Dionysos (*ex machina*) announced the foundation of his cult for all at Thebes. This would be in line with the founding of *polis* cult by a deity (*ex machina*) at the end of many other Euripidean plays. And the very last line of the play (1388-92 are spurious) mentions future maenadism in Mt. Kithairon. The problem is that part of his final speech is lost, and it was in these lost lines that - I regard it as virtually certain - he announced the foundation of his cult. This would accord with the hypothesis (ancient plot-summary) of the play, which says that Dionysos in this speech "announced some things for everybody" (surely in this section he announced the cult) and to each individual made clear what will happen to them (part of this final section survives).

The issue is complicated by the *Christus Patiens*, a

mediaeval dramatic cento of about 2,600 lines on the passion of Christ, put together from various sources. It seems that about 300 lines of it are influenced by the *Bacchae*. Nowhere does it refer to the founding of Dionysiac cult in Thebes, and some lines in it have been taken to show that Dionysos imposed collective exile on the Thebans as punishment for rejecting his cult. Murray printed some lines of the *Christus Patiens* at the end of his Oxford Classical Text of the *Bacchae*; and Dodds in his *Commentary* on the play added a few more in an Appendix, and took as evidence some lines from the *Christus Patiens* in his astonishingly uncritical note on what has been lost after line 1329. The matter needs further investigation.

Of the 300 relevant lines of *Christus Patiens*, most have been adapted to the Christian context, often heavily. Only 17 of them are identical to lines in the *Bacchae*. There is no reason why the founding of Dionysiac cult should have been reproduced in the *Christus Patiens*. Moreover, there is nothing either in the *Bacchae* or in the *Christus Patiens* to suggest that the Thebans as a whole rejected Dionysos or that he blamed them or imposed collective exile on them. This is hardly surprising, because the cult of himself founded by Dionysos at Thebes would, had the Thebans been exiled, have had nobody to celebrate it. *Christus Patiens* lines 1668-9 say that the people must leave the city. But even if these lines were influenced by *Bacchae*, it would be entirely within the spirit of the *Christus Patiens* to have substituted *laon* (the people) for Kadmon (like the substitution of Adam for Kadmon at *Christus Patiens* 193). The exile of a whole *polis* is alien to the spirit of Greek tragedy. Only in Aeschylus' *Persians* and Euripides' *Trojan Women* in extant tragedy does a whole community suffer in the the end, and in neither case is the community Greek (for his *Sack of Miletus* Phrynichus was fined). What seems likely is that the author of the *Christus Patiens*, interested in the collective guilt and and consequent exile (*diaspora*) of the Jews, found nothing comparable in Greek tragedy, and so had to adapt the exile of the Theban royal family. I have set out this argument in more detail in *Arion* 8. 2 (2000) 86-91.

The result of the *Bacchae* then is the destruction (or self-destruction) of the ruling family, and collective benefit for the *polis*. Even poor old Kadmos had to leave. To be sure, he had espoused the new cult, but perhaps only in order to benefit his own family (333-6). And he was after all a member of the ruling family, being - as he makes very clear in his funerary praise of Pentheus - Pentheus' grandfather. The important point is that Euripides and his audience may have felt pity and awe at the fates of Pentheus, Agaue, and Kadmos while welcoming the egalitarian effect of Dionysos in the *polis*.

Putting Together the Pieces: a Passage in the *Bacchae*

Pat Easterling

Nearly one-fifth of Euripides' total output has survived: a record for a Greek tragedian and a remarkable fact if one stops to reflect that these texts had to be copied and re-copied by hand for 1900 years before they reached the comparative safety of print. In his own time Eruipides was a writer who aroused strong feelings, both for and against. By shocking, teasing and unsettling his audiences he tried to make them think critically, which was not always comfortable; but later generations found his 'modernity' and subversiveness easier to cope with and rated him higher than Aeschylus or Sophocles. Of the plays that have come through to us some were popular classics in late antiquity, periodically revived on stage and used as the ancient equivalent of set books in schools, while others were less famous and survived more or less by accident.

Through one of the many quirks in this long process of transmission our surviving text of the *Bacchae*, which we know was one of Euripides' most celebrated plays, has been damaged on its way: in two places near the end a whole section of a speech or dialogue has dropped out. We can tell roughly when this happened and even guess how. The text was still complete until some date in the early middle ages (or possibly later), because an anonymous Christian who composed a play called *Christ in his Passion* (*Christus Patiens*) borrowed extensively from the *Bacchae* for his own play, using whole lines from the story of Pentheus torn apart by maenads to describe the sufferings of Christ – a procedure which might have surprised even Euripides. But by the early fourteenth century, the date when our one surviving complete manuscript was copied, the damage had already been done.

The easiest explanation of how the text became defective is that the Bacchae was the last play in a volume, and that the volume was unbound: just as the first few and last few pages of a paperback are the ones most easily damaged, so with its medieval equivalent. Probably one or two pages were detached and lost, leaving scholars with the job of filling in the gaps as well as they could. As it happens, reconstructing the lost passages is more than a mildly interesting detective operation: it raises issues of real importance for our understanding of the play. I shall concentrate here on the first of the gaps, which occurs well on in the final scene.

Agave and Pentheus

Agave, the mother of the young king Pentheus, has come back from what to her has been a profoundly thrilling experience on the mountainside: she has been up there in the wilds with a band of Theban women, taking part in ecstatic worship which has culminated in the hunting down and tearing apart of a young lion, and now she is bringing home the creature's head as her trophy. Or so she believes. In fact, as the Chorus and the audience can see, it is her own son's head that she carries, and Agave is in a state of mad delusion, which has been induced by Dionysus himself because she and her sisters rejected the story of his divine birth. Pentheus, too, has rejected the god and has paid the horrendous penalty of death and dismemberment.

Agave is soon joined by her father Cadmus and his attendants, who carry the remains of Pentheus, carefully gathered together and brought down from the mountain:

> *CADMUS: Follow me, servants, carrying the sad weight of Pentheus; bring it here, in front of the palace. I am returning with his body after laborious and endless search: it was torn to pieces in the glens of Cithaeron, and I found nothing in the same place, but it all lay scattered in the tangled woods. (1215–21)*

In a scene of intense pathos Cadmus gradually brings Agave back to her senses and helps her to understand what it is that she is holding. Agave now needs to discover how Pentheus was killed and to find out what has happened to the rest of his corpse. Lines 1298–1300 seem to be leading up to a dramatic climax in which she laments over the dead Pentheus and returns the head to the body. They run like this:

> *AGAVE: And the beloved body of my son, where is it, father?*
> *CADMUS: Here – I am bringing it. I searched it out with difficulty.*
> *AGAVE: Is it all fitted together in decent fashion, limb to limb?*

But in our text as it stands there is no answer from Cadmus, no lamentation on Agave's part, and no indication of what she does with Pentheus' head.

A gap in the puzzle

This must be where we meet the first gap: we have evidence from elsewhere, partly from lines quoted in the *Christus Patiens* and particularly from a résumé of this scene in the work of Apsines, a rhetorician of the third century A.D., that Agave did lament over her son's body, and the speech of Cadmus that follows in our text (1302ff) sounds like a sort of funeral oration, praising the good qualities of the young king, which would come appropriately after the lamentation. This is how Apsines summarises the missing sequence:

> In Euripides, Pentheus' mother Agave, recovered from her madness and recognising that it is her own child who has been torn to pieces, accuses herself and arouses pity.

> Euripides succeeds in arousing pity for Pentheus like this: his mother, holding each of his limbs in her hands, laments them one by one.

Does what Apsines says imply that the putting together, piece by piece, of Pentheus' body was recalled on stage, with Agave picking up and addressing each part in turn? Many critics have been very uneasy with this idea of putting together the pieces (W.S. Barrett called it a 'grisly jigsaw') and typically they have wanted to limit the stage action to the minimum – just the replacement of Pentheus' head on his body. But it would be a mistake to think we can decide on grounds of taste – modern taste – what an ancient Athenian audience would and would not have accepted. What strikes us as grotesque sensationalism might have seemed perfectly serious and proper to them. Could the emphasis on the piecing together of Pentheus have had some function not immediately obvious to us?

Three other scenarios

One way of answering this question is to think of and rule out alternative scenarios. Three possibilities suggest themselves. The body could have been lost, the pieces irrecoverably scattered on the mountainside and never put together at all. Or it could have been eaten by the maenads: in Dionysiac worship, after all, the *sparagmos* (tearing apart) was regularly followed by *ômophagia* (eating raw), and Agave in her madness invites the Chorus to 'share the meal' when she comes back from her 'hunt' (1184). Or it could have been reassembled only in part: Seneca's *Phaedra* ends with a scene in which Theseus laments over the dead Hippolytus, whose broken body is never completely put together. In that play emphasis is repeatedly laid on the impossibility of full recomposition: the Chorus, for example, recognise some of the pieces, but exclaim 'How large a part is still lacking to our tears' (1261), and Theseus is perplexed as he tries to reassemble the fragments:

> *What is this shapeless, ugly piece, with wounds on every side? I do not know what part of you it is, but it is a part of you. Here, set it here: not in its own but in a vacant place.* (1267–9)

Even after he has given instructions for the preparation of the funeral fire he tells his servants to go out and look for stray pieces of the body.

We know that the first two of these options were definitely not chosen by Euripides, and there are strong reasons for thinking that the third would not have suited him either. Cadmus' words (quoted above) as he returns with the remains that he has carefully collected, and Agave's concern to know whether they have been properly put together, seem to be leading to a scene in which Pentheus is restored to the status of a human being receiving his due of mourning – no longer a wild beast or a mass of shapeless fragments. There has been time for such horror, which has been lavishly expressed in the messenger's speech in such lines 1135–6: 'And all the women had blood-stained hands as they played ball with the pieces of Pentheus' flesh'. But what is needed now is an emotional and ritual context in which Cadmus' 'funeral oration' praising Pentheus as king and grandson will seem appropriate. And the extraordinary dramatic potential of the main stage property, the head, must be exploited.

The 'funeral' of Pentheus

Perhaps we should see the reassembling of Pentheus, and particularly the return of the head to the body, as a gesture of reintegration, the only one that the play offers: reintegration in terms of ritual order, not as any kind of promise of regeneration or as any kind of solution to the problems posed by the play, but important for the response it makes to the overwhelming horror of what has happened. Human beings, the *Bacchae* suggests, are at the mercy of forces inside nature, and inside themselves, that are liable to destroy them; the only means they have of coping, or trying to cope, with such violence is through the institutions of society, which depend on carefully observed ritual action. Perverted, this can be disastrous, as when the women on the mountains tear Pentheus apart, but it can also provide the context for expressing the essential values of human society in the face of suffering and death.

Giving Pentheus the right funeral is enormously important. Here, although Agave as her son's murderess is presumably excluded from the burial rites and soon will be banished from Thebes by Dionysus, she can take part in the crucial lamentation, so that what happens on stage marks the beginning of Pentheus' funeral, which Cadmus will complete. At the very end of the play we should imagine Cadmus and his attendants moving off with the bier. In many modern productions the remains of Pentheus are left lying onstage, as though that were the end of the story, but the clear indication of Euripides' text is surely that Cadmus will complete the ritual he has begun.

Dionysiac ritual

There is a further point to be made about the reassembling of Pentheus and what it could have meant. In Euripides' time Dionysus was worshipped in rites of all kinds, including one in which the women roamed the mountains (in a probably much tamer version of the activities described in the *Bacchae*), as well as in festivals in which the main focus was on wine, as in the Anthesteria, or on dramatic performances, as in the Dionysia and Lenaea. But he was also by this time the centre of a mystery cult, comparable to that of Demeter at Eleusis, but not focused like the Eleusinian Mysteries on one particular sacred site. Groups of Dionysiac initiates could worship anywhere, as archaeological evidence has shown. We are left guessing about many of the details because mysteries were by definition secret, but so far as we can tell, in some versions of the myth that formed the basis of the cult the child Dionysus was dismembered, and his limbs were collected by his mother so that he could be brought back to life; and the initiands probably experienced some pattern of ritual that mimicked this death and rebirth. Now Pentheus may indeed be the opposite of the true initiate – as the god's enemy who is *not* reborn – but this story could have been felt to have more significance the more closely it echoed the mystic story of Dionysus.

Of course we have no means of telling how large a proportion of the audience would know enough about the Dionysiac mysteries to see the play in mystic terms, that is, as offering some special reassurance to those who were in closest touch with Dionysus' power. To many modern readers the *Bacchae* seems peculiarly frightening, with its emphasis on the implacability of Dionysus towards the human beings who have offended him. Our sense of the matter is more likely to be that *all* the people involved suffer far worse than they deserve, and that the main point is the cruelty shown by the god.

Nothing can reduce the sense of tragic loss conveyed by the end of the play, as Agave says farewell to her father and prepares to go into exile, but Greek religious thinking had no difficulty in accommodating gods who were both destructive and benign (Euripides' Dionysus calls himself 'most terrible and most gentle' 861). Even if the mystic reference is only a glancing hint and very far from being the main focus of the tragedy, at least it can perhaps offer us some sort of clue when we try to understand how the *Bacchae* could be composed for performance at a festival expressly designed to honour Dionysus. It might also help to explain why a Christian writer could find raw material here for a different kind of sacred story.

This is a slightly revised version of an article first published in *Omnibus* 14, November 1987

The Paradox of the *Bacchae*

Alex Garvie

Bacchae is a play of paradoxes – the paradox of an oriental god who brings his religion from Asia to Greece, and yet was born to Zeus and Semele in Thebes; the paradox of a new religious cult which Tiresias will claim to be as old as time itself; the paradox of a choral entrance-song whose theme is the cult of an oriental god, yet which takes the form of a traditional Greek hymn; the paradox of Dionysus as a god whose cult proclaims blessedness only for those initiated into his Mysteries, but who is also the god of the ordinary man, and who demands worship from everybody, irrespective of their gender or their age; the paradox of an ecstatic religion which requires moderation and good sense in its practitioners. This essay will concentrate on the most striking paradox of all. The god who throughout the play promises joy will at the end produce only suffering and horror.

We meet Dionysus first in the prologue. He explains to us how he has travelled from Asia to introduce his new religion to Thebes. But his aunts deny his divinity and, with all the women, have been driven mad into the mountains, where they are sitting peacefully under the silver-fir trees, while Pentheus, the young king of Thebes, is resisting the new religion. Dionysus therefore plans to manifest himself to Pentheus and to the whole of Thebes, before moving on to some other land. The tone is unemotional and factual. All the emphasis is on the manifestation of Dionysus' divinity, and there is not a word about punishment for Pentheus, little to rouse either our sympathy for the god or our disapproval of his plan. Before he departs he explains that he has disguised himself as a human votary of himself. Only at the end of the play will he appear again in his divine form.

If the tone of the prologue is unemotional, that of the chorus's entrance-song is quite the reverse. This is indeed one of the most exciting entrance-songs in the whole of Greek tragedy. The irruption of the oriental god into Greece is represented for us by the chorus of his oriental followers, who have travelled with him from Asia, as they irrupt into the theatre, dancing wildly and singing in emotional rhythms, to the accompaniment of drums. The keynote of the song is the blessedness of the initiates, and the exciting joy of going to the mountain to dance in ecstasy. Note the recurring ritual cry, "to the mountain, to the mountain". If this is what Dionysiac worship means, how can anyone be against it? At this early stage we hardly notice the single brief reference to the more violent aspect of the cult, the joy of hunting a goat and eating it raw. And, if we have some faint misgivings about the escapism that it involves (the women on the mountain have abandoned their housework!), they are entirely overshadowed by the overall mood of joy. We are certainly not yet encouraged to think about what will come back from the mountain at the end of the play. The chorus will play a vital part in this tragedy, as it guides our emotional reaction. Joy will be the theme of most of its songs, but, as was shown in a study published forty years ago, there will be a progressive degradation in its understanding of that joy.

We have noted the dramatic change in mood between prologue and entrance-song. Equally striking is the reversal of mood between entrance-song and the following episode. The aged prophet Tiresias arrives on stage to summon the equally aged Cadmus, the grandfather of Pentheus, so that they can go off to the mountain to worship. Clad in Dionysiac fawn-skins, carrying Dionysiac wands (*thyrsoi*), and wearing ivy-garlands on their heads, they look forward to taking part in the wild dancing on the mountain, claiming that they alone in Thebes have good sense. Cadmus calls Tiresias "wise", but what is the relationship between rational wisdom and the demands of this emotional religion? Does one not have to be "mad" to join in Dionysiac dancing? They are joyful because they have forgotten their old age, and feel that they can dance all night and day. The irrational is not confined to any one age-group, but there is something a little ridiculous about the spectacle, and the mood descends almost into bathos when Cadmus, despite his claim to be rejuvenated, asks pathetically if they cannot go to the mountain on a carriage.

So far we have seen Dionysus through our own eyes and through the eyes of his followers. But now we are to see him through the eyes of Pentheus, his principal antagonist. Pentheus in his opening speech makes clear his reasons for opposing this new religion: it is merely a pretext for luring women into the mountains to indulge in illicit sexual unions. He mocks the effeminate appearance of the supposed votary. Like a typical stage-tyrant he thinks that violence is the solution to all problems, and plans to hunt down and imprison the women on the mountain. Tiresias and Cadmus do their best to persuade Pentheus to change his mind, Tiresias by means of a number of sophistic arguments, which no doubt justify Cadmus' description of him as intellectually "wise", but which leave out entirely the excitement of the chorus's entrance-song. Joy has now become the pleasure of drinking wine, which helps one to sleep and to forget one's troubles. Dionysus *is* the god of wine, so there is nothing false about this argument. But

Dionysus is so much more besides, and, after the excitement of the entrance-song, Tiresias' defence of the new religion is clearly inadequate. When he accuses Pentheus of being mad, he forgets that madness is an essential part of Dionysiac religion. Cadmus' justification for worshipping the god is even less satisfactory: even if Dionysus is not a god, it will be good for the honour of the family to pretend that he is. He accuses Pentheus of having no good sense, the quality on which the two old men have prided themselves. It is hardly surprising that by the end of the episode Pentheus remains unconvinced, and departs with orders to his men to arrest the votary and bring him back to face execution by stoning.

The choral song which follows deals again with Dionysiac joy, but gone now is all the excitement of the entrance-song. The chorus takes its cue from the arguments of Tiresias, and presents Dionysus in conventional terms as essentially the god of wine and of peaceful convivial parties. The ode is full of the commonplaces of Greek thought. Moderation and wisdom are praised, and the wisdom is that of the common man. Again we feel that there is something lacking. At the beginning of the next episode we are suddenly reminded of what the ode omitted. Enter a servant with the "votary" under arrest. The servant describes how Pentheus' men "hunted down" their prey, and here now is the "animal" which they have caught. The metaphor foreshadows the way in which Dionysus, at this stage of the play the prey, will later turn into the hunter of Pentheus. So begins the first of three confrontations between the god and Pentheus. It ends with Pentheus apparently in control, as the votary is led off to prison in the palace-stables. But already we have a sense that the god is merely playing with him.

In the next choral ode Dionysus is again seen as a god of wine. The chorus cannot understand why Thebes rejects the joy which he brings, and calls on him, not yet to punish, nor to take vengeance on, Pentheus, but merely to put a stop to his outrageous behaviour (*hybris*). The song is interrupted by the voice offstage of Dionysus, who is miraculously released from his prison, and who now appears on stage to describe how he sat quietly as Pentheus rushed around in a futile attempt to bind a bull, which he mistook for the votary. Given that Dionysus has already been described in the entrance-song of the chorus as the "bull-horned god", it is a pardonable error. Enter Pentheus, totally bewildered by the escape of his prisoner. He is closely followed by a herdsman, who, in the first of two formal messenger-speeches in this play, has come to report the behaviour of the women on the mountain. At first all is peaceful and idyllic, but the mood soon changes. The herdsman and shepherds set out to "hunt" the women, as a pleasant sport. But it is the women who hunt the hunters. They tear the cattle in pieces with their bare hands, and the fragments are hanging from the trees dripping with blood. For the first time in the play the keynote is violence, but as yet the principal victims are animals, not human beings. The women go on to raid the neighbouring villages, and succeed in wounding men. But this detail is passed over lightly, and the women finally return to the peace of the mountain. Violence and peace are juxtaposed, and it is left to the messenger to draw a wholly inadequate moral: this is a powerful god, who has given us the vine which stops our pain – without wine there is no pleasure for men.

Pentheus, failing totally to appreciate the power of his antagonist, resolves to lead his army against the women on the mountain. But Dionysus, in the second confrontation between the two, offers instead to take him, with no army, to spy on the women. First, however, he must put on female clothes, so that he may remain undetected. Pentheus at first recoils, but it is clear that he really wants to see the women engaged in their immoral activities, and, although he pretends, as he leaves the stage, that he has not yet made his decision, we know that it is in fact already taken, and that he is already lost. After his departure Dionysus has his last word. It remains for him only to make his enemy mad. Pentheus is heading for a hunter's net. For the first time in the play we are explicitly told that he is to be punished, and that death will be his punishment. But first he must become a laughing-stock for all the Thebans, as he walks through the city dressed in female clothes. The last line of Dionysus' speech sums up the paradox of this religion, "a god most terrible, but most gentle to mankind".

The choral song that follows begins with a sense of movement and excitement that we have not heard from the chorus since its entrance-song. It looks forward to its joy, when, like a fawn that has escaped from the hunting-nets, it will be fully free to worship the god. But the sense of excitement does not last. Soon we return to the platitudes of Greek thought, and the joy at the end of the ode has deteriorated into that of momentary pleasures: "that man whose life is happy day by day, him I call blessed". The third confrontation between Dionysus and Pentheus is the most unpleasant. Pentheus, now completely under the god's control, totally destroyed from a psychological point of view, and giggling as he fusses about his hair and the fall of his woman's dress, sets off happily with Dionysus to see the sexual activities of the women on the mountain. It is not a pretty sight. His last words are "I am getting what I deserve". If till now we were not sure whether or not to sympathise with Pentheus, there can no longer be any doubt.

The following choral ode is the most exciting since the entrance-song, and, unlike the previous ode, there is no diminution of that excitement at the end. The chorus call on the swift hunting-dogs of Madness to go to the mountain, to incite the women to take vengeance on the man who has gone to the mountain to seek them out. "I enjoy hunting", they say. Pentheus, the hunter, is to become the victim of the hunt. The manifestation of justice (cf. the theme of manifestation in the prologue) is now unequivocally identified with the killing of Pentheus. Finally the chorus call on Dionysus to appear in his bestial form, as a bull or a serpent or a lion, and with smiling face to cast a noose round his victim. The violence which was merely hinted at in the entrance-song is now uppermost in our minds.

This is the cue for the appearance of the second Messenger, who comes to announce Pentheus' death. The chorus-leader's first, triumphant, reaction dismays the Messenger. "What are you saying? Do you really rejoice at my masters' misfortunes, lady?…It is not right to rejoice at the evil things that have been done". In a full-scale formal messenger-speech he describes for us these evil things. The climax comes when the mad Agave, Pentheus' mother, ignores her, now sane, son's appeal for pity, and, together with the other women, tears him limb from limb. She is now on her way back from the mountain, carrying Pentheus' head in triumph on her thyrsus, "priding herself on her hunt", in her delusion thinking that it is the head of a lion. This, then, is what Dionysiac joy has become, the joy of a mother who has killed her son. The Messenger ends with a moral that is as banal as that which concluded the earlier messenger-speech: "Moderation and respect for the things of the gods are best; I think that this is also the wisest possession for mortals who practise it". The gulf between the platitude and the horror of what the Messenger has reported is very striking.

In a brief lyric passage the chorus maintains the triumphant tone. And then Agave enters, carrying her grisly burden from the mountain, to join the chorus in a highly emotional lyric dialogue. The themes of joy and hunting continue to be interwoven, but there is a telling moment when even the chorus, till now completely sympathetic to Dionysus and hostile to Pentheus, expresses revulsion at Agave's invitation to join her in eating the raw flesh of the "lion". Cadmus reappears, carrying the pieces of Pentheus' body which he has gathered on the mountain. At first his grief contrasts with Agave's continuing joy. But Cadmus begins the process of enlightening her. At first she tries to evade the truth, feeling perhaps instinctively that she can remain happy only as long as she is still mad. But eventually she is forced to accept it, and the joy is gone for ever: "Alas, what do I see? What is this that I am carrying in my hands?…Unhappy me, I see a most painful thing!" And the cause of her suffering is clear to her: "Dionysus has destroyed us, as now I understand." Cadmus sums it up: "Wretched am I, miserable are you [Pentheus], pitiable your mother, miserable your relations".

At the end of the play there is no joy for anyone. Even the chorus has found it too much to bear. It is the punishment of Cadmus which seems most unfair, as even the chorus-leader acknowledges: "your grandson has the punishment which he deserved, but it is painful for you". He who set off for the mountain to worship Dionysus, not indeed for the best of motives, suffers as much as anyone else. We may suppose that this is merely a case of the innocent suffering along with the guilty, but that is not exactly how Euripides presents it. The manuscripts break off after the chorus-leader's expression of sympathy, and, when they resume, Dionysus is on stage, no longer in disguise, in the middle of a speech, prophesying that Cadmus is to be transformed into a snake and driven into exile. "If you [plural – he includes Cadmus in the whole family] had known how to show good sense (or "moderation"), when you did not want to, you would have been happy, having acquired the son of Zeus [i.e. Dionysus himself] as ally". Cadmus might, we feel, have replied that he had indeed done his best to behave in the manner that Dionysus now recommends, and that what he has learnt is that moderation and good sense are the last things that are required in the worshipper of this god. Instead, he concedes that "we have done you wrong", and complains only that Dionysus has gone too far in his vengeance. "Gods", he says, "should not be like mortals in their tempers". The trouble is that they are. Scholars used to argue about whether in this play Euripides is arguing in favour of Dionysiac religion, or, on the contrary, that the god does not deserve to be worshipped, if he exists at all. Most critics now recognise that to put the question in these terms is mistaken. The power of the irrational, which Dionysus represents, does undoubtedly exist, and there is no point in saying that one is either against or in favour of it.

Is there any hope at all at the end of the play? We might like to suppose that Dionysus drives mad only those who reject his divinity, and that if we worship him properly he will bring us only joy. But the play gives us little guidance as to what his proper worship would be. Cadmus, who did his best, suffers with the rest, and even the chorus has its moment of revulsion. The comfort that Cadmus and Agave offer each other is only temporary; for, as the play ends, they depart to their separate exile. Richard Seaford, the most recent editor of the play, in an interesting interpretation, sees the suffering as a necessary prelude to the foundation of Dionysus' civic and communal cult in Thebes. The royal family had to destroy itself and be driven out before the city could begin to practise it. Pentheus is thus to be seen as a kind of scapegoat whose destruction benefits the whole city. It is true that in the prologue Dionysus announces his intention of manifesting himself to all the people of Thebes, and we might expect the effect on the community to play some part at the end of the play. But, as we have it, nothing at all is said about it. This may be why the loss of part of the final scene in the manuscripts is so disastrous; for it may be there that this optimistic idea was developed. All that we can safely say, however, is that in the play as it stands there is no optimism at all at the end. And, even if the interpretation of the lacuna is correct, it is surely the horror that predominates. Somehow the despair seems all the darker because of the recurring theme of joy that has preceded it. The play was written in monarchic Macedonia, but presented in democratic Athens, in the theatre of Dionysus, as part of the god's festival. He is the patron god of tragedy as well as comedy. His concern is with suffering as well as laughter. He may bring joy, but the potential for that joy to turn to tragedy is always present.

The two works referred to in this essay are:

J. de Romilly, "Le Thème du bonheur dans les Bacchantes", *Revue des études grecques* 76 (1963) 361-80

R. Seaford, *Euripides, Bacchae: with an introduction, translation and commentary* (Warminster 1996)

aod publications

Further collections of essays on the following plays are also available:

Aeschylus   *Agamemnon*

Euripides   *Trojan Women*

In addition, our series "*Dionysus*" contains transcripts of pre-performance talks on the following plays:

Aeschylus   *Agamemnon*
                    Choephoroi

Sophocles   *Ajax*
                    Antigone
                    Oedipus the King

Euripides   *Bacchae*
                    Electra
                    Hippolytus
                    Medea
                    Trojan Women

For information about any of these, as well as translations, adaptations, audiobooks, videos and dvds, please contact:

actors of dionysus ltd,
14 cuthbert road, brighton, uk bn2 0en
tel/fax +0044 1273 692 604   e info@actorsofdionysus.com
www.actorsofdionysus.com